YOUR KNOWLEDGE HAS VALUE

AF137956

- We will publish your bachelor's and master's thesis, essays and papers

- Your own eBook and book - sold worldwide in all relevant shops

- Earn money with each sale

Upload your text at www.GRIN.com
and publish for free

Bibliographic information published by the German National Library:

The German National Library lists this publication in the National Bibliography;
detailed bibliographic data are available on the Internet at http://dnb.dnb.de .

Imprint:

Copyright © 2015 GRIN Verlag, Open Publishing GmbH
Print and binding: Books on Demand GmbH, Norderstedt Germany
ISBN: 978-3-668-04352-7

This book at GRIN:

http://www.grin.com/en/e-book/306329/access-to-basic-sports-facilities-in-india-a-
survey-of-12-universities

Kusum lata, Sneh lata, Manoj Kumar

Access to basic sports facilities in India. A survey of 12 universities in Haryana

GRIN Publishing

GRIN - Your knowledge has value

Since its foundation in 1998, GRIN has specialized in publishing academic texts by students, college teachers and other academics as e-book and printed book. The website www.grin.com is an ideal platform for presenting term papers, final papers, scientific essays, dissertations and specialist books.

Visit us on the internet:

http://www.grin.com/

http://www.facebook.com/grincom

http://www.twitter.com/grin_com

Access to basic sports facilities in India. A survey of 12 universities in Haryana

Sneh lata[1], Kusum Lata[2] and Manoj Kumar[3]

ABSTRACT

The present study is an attempt to know the perception of university students regarding the access of basic sports facilities in Haryana. A survey targeting youths is conducted in 12 UGC recognized universities in Haryana in which 11 are State Universities and 1 is Central University. Total sample size of present study is 432 university students of these universities. After a pilot study was done, 432 questionnaires were administered to the targeted respondents aged between16-30years & above, using combination of purposive and random sampling techniques. The study found that there is a significant difference between gender and accessibility of sports facilities such as the availability of healthy diet, accessibility of playing equipment on time as well as the quality of the available equipment, accessibility and quality of medical facilities, coaching facility, coaching time and quality, team selection etc.

[1] PhD Research Scholar, Department of Political Science, Central University of Haryana, Mahendergarh

[2] Extension Lecturer, Department of Political Science, Government College for Girls sec-14 Gurgaon

[3] Assistant Professor, Department of Economics, Central University of Haryana, Mahendergarh.

INTRODUCTION

Haryana is counted among the prosperous states of India. Statistical way of measurements, attribute high performance in sports to five factors: population, per capita income, past performance, climate and host-effect. Haryana has advantages on these counts. Besides, the State is among the top performers in the country indicated by developmental indicators and maintained it gradually.

In addition to this, Haryana state has a youthful demographic profile. As per 2001 census, 48 percent population is lying in the age bracket of 10-35 years. The people particularly younger, energetic, aware and amenable are mobilized. Sports and games are an integral part of human life and important for human resources development. They are also an effective way to channelize the energy of youth in productive and meaningful purposes. The State Government has therefore accorded a high priority to provide incentives in the State. With a vision to make Haryana a vibrant leading edge State in the Sports arena; by Universalization Sports Infrastructure throughout the length and breadth of State; Unearth latest Sports talents in Youth and lead them towards peaks of Sports Excellence. A sports policy was framed in the year 2001 and revised in the year 2009.

The policy was revisited and updated in the year 2012, and now in April, 2013, to increase the cash awards and incentives. Time to time different revised policies are taking places for sports persons, cash awards for Olympics and Para-Olympic Games 2016 have been doubled, and honoraria sanctioned for Dronacharya, Arjuna and Dhyan Chand awardees. Haryana added financial incentives, greater declaration of an assured future; and still greater stimulus to deliver more and better. What does Haryana proud is that the Central Government has taken a leaf out of its book and decided to set up rural sports stadia in 28 states and four UTs.[4] It is really done wonder, changed the tiny entity of federal India from a sports nursery to sports motivating force. And put the state on global sporting hessian. And recently it wants to bring Right to Play Act[5] to make the State a model in sports promotion.

Haryana has a strong culture of sports. In last few years Haryana has been making national headlines for good reasons though it consists merely 2% of India's population. Among the 81 members of the Indian contingent at London 2012, 18 hail from Haryana. Leaving out MC Mary Kom and Vijay Kumar, the other four medallists from London are either from Haryana or have their roots there. During the 2010 Commonwealth Games in New Delhi, Haryana contributed no less than 22 of the 38 gold medals that India won at the Games. Athletes from Haryana clinched 37 of the 101 medals won by India. In recent Glasgove CWG 2014 also Haryanvi players keep their name high.

Sports and Physical Aptitude Tests (SPAT) have been introduced by Haryana government. And recently it wants to bring Right to Play Act to make the State a model in sports promotion.

---

[4] Haryana review june 2013

[5] Times of India, oct.17, 2012

REVIEW OF RELATED LITERATURE

Bhupendra Yadav (2012) in his article 'Why Haryana is India's mine for medals' said that it is somewhere because Haryana is a Jaat land, which is considered as a martial race (hardworking). All sports are concerned with the Olympic slogan 'higher, faster and stronger'. He tried to find out the reasons behind why Haryana perform better in game with aggression like wrestling, boxing. He claimed that there are three reasons for it, viz. firstly, this state has a volatile history of constant aggression due to its geographical position on the frontier. Secondly, he observed that the people of Haryana have appreciated physical strength due to its peasant culture. Thirdly, the author affirms that the sports policy 2006 of Haryana has honed the killer athletic spirit. The Haryana government since 2006, has decided to help directly to its athletes. The players who excels in sports get cash rewards and government jobs through sports quota. The author criticized the sports policy of Haryana by saying that it does not help create champions or to build a sports culture. The sports policy only helps the famous and supports the successful.

Ahlawat, Ravinder, (2011) this study aims to investigate the role of school in sports participation. Using the purposive sampling method, the investigator select 50 school administrator as sample and collect the data with the help of structured questionnaire. The study findings revealed that more than 92% of the respondents believe that physical education and sports participation contributes to the holistic development of the children as well in making them a good citizen.

Sangwan, Jagmati, (2008) in her study titled 'Participation of Women in Sports: A Case Study of International Sportswomen with Special Reference to Haryana State' tried to identify the contribution of Haryana's female sportsperson in sports as well as the obstacles faced by them during their participation. Using the case study method the investigator collect the data with the help of structured questionnaire and focused interview schedule. The researcher found in her study that negative image of sports and sports women that works as a hindrance to the participation

Malik, Sanjit, (2008) in his doctoral thesis on 'A Study of Socio- Economic Status and Level of Aspiration Affecting the Performance of North Indian Wrestlers' aims to find the role played by social as well as economic factors in sports participation and in sports performance at various level of participation. The investigator chooses 200 senior sector freestyle north Indian wrestlers who participated in international or position in National and inter- university tournament as sample. The investigator found positive and significant relationship between socio- economic conditions and sports participation as well as performance in tournaments.

Chahal,Vinod, (2002) in his research on 'Critical Analysis of Female Participation in Sports with Special Reference to Haryana State' observed the present position of female sports participation as well as women's attitude towards sports and the myths that exist in the society regarding sports participation. The study covering the four district of Haryana state namely Hisar, Rohtak, Karnal and Sonipat with the total sample size of 200 participants ranging between the age group of 14-19 years of various schools and colleges. The study revealed that attitude of women participation in sports is not considered as good as the male sports participation. The investigator also found that participation in sports and physical activities may create hurdle in marriage as well as child bearing of the women sportsperson.

Vaz, M. and A.V. Bharathi in their article on 'Perceptions of the Intensity of Specific Physical Activities in Bangalore, South India: Implications for Exercise Prescription' tried to assess the perceptions of the intensity of specifics sports activities in urban area of India. The investigators used a structured questionnaire and self-administered it to convenience sample of 782 adults in which 441 was aged between 17 to 70 years in Bangalore city. The findings of this study show that the intensity rated of female are significantly higher than male in case intensity of jogging, manual labour and walking uphill.

OBJECTIVE OF THE STUDY

1. To know the perception of university students regarding the access of basic sports facilities in Haryana

HYPOTHESIS

H0 There is no relationship between gender identity and access to basic sports facilities.

H1 There is significant relationship between gender identity and access to basic sports facilities.

METHODOLOGY

Quantitative methodology was used in this study. According to Sarantakos (1998) one of the most important qualities of quantitative research is the requirement that the sample employed reflects the attributes of the target population. Therefore, the finding it produces relates to the whole population, and the conclusions drawn through the study is pertinent to the whole population.

Area of Study

The area of present study is Haryana State. Haryana emerged as a separate State on November 1, 1966. According to the census of 2011, the total population of Haryana is about 25 million. Haryana lies in the northern region of the country. It is well linked to the national capital and most of the area of Haryana state is under NCR.. The total geographical area of Haryana state is spread over about 44000sq. km which makes it 20th largest state of the country in terms of area.

Why Haryana

Haryana is ideal because of its cosmopolitan nature and it is possible to find representation of the desired population from other parts of the country. The area of study has good connectivity to the National Capital, so the availability of resources is relatively higher. The large area is of this state is under NCR so that population is highly educated and urbanized. According to the 2011 census data, the Literacy rate in Haryana is 75.55% (in which male literacy rate stands at 84.06% while female literacy rate is at 56.915). Sex Ratio of Haryana state is 879 female on 1000 male, which is below the national average of 940 as per 2011 census data. Secondly, in Haryana there are significant number of public and private universities and colleges (students) which are targeted for this study. This study is targeting the youth who are actively or non actively participated in sports, Haryana provides the best access to this group. Haryana is the most prosperous among states in India. It is the only state which has having one of the highest per capita income in the country,6

Target Population

Total target population is 43436 university students studying in Haryana in various UGC recognized universities in which 24645 are male and 18791 are female according to the data available on the UGC website for the session 2011-12.

---

6 http://www.census2011.co.in/census/state/haryana.html

4

Sample Size

Total sample size of the present study 432 students (Male= 198 and Female= 234) students' studying in 12 UGC recognized universities in Haryana state.

DATA INTERPRETATION & RESULTS

RESPONDENTS PROFILE

Age and Gender of the respondents are the most important characteristics in understanding their views about the particular problems. Higher age indicates level of maturity of individuals in that sense age becomes more important to examine the response.

Table 1 Distribution by Age Group & Gender

Age Group of the Respondents	Gender		Total	Percentage
	Female	Male		
16-20 Years	122	21	143	33.1
21-25 Years	86	109	195	45.1
26-30 Years	25	61	86	19.9
30 Years & Above	1	7	8	1.9
Total	**234**	**198**	**432**	**100.0**

Table-1 represents age wise and gender wise composition of the respondents. 143 respondents out of 432 belong to the age group of 16-20 years of which 21 are male and 122 are female. While 109 of male and 86 of females are belongs to the age group of 21-25 years. And a further 61 of male and 25 of female are comes under the age group of 26-30 years and 7 male and 1 female respondents respectively are between the age group of 30 years and above. The data shows that majority of surveyed respondents (195) are belongs to 21-25 years age group which is much higher number than other age group.

MEASURING THE VARIABLE: ACCESS TO SPORTS FACILITIES

To tap the basic sports facilities several questions were asked to the respondents related to availability of balance diet, playing equipments, quality of available equipment, coaching facilities, training time, playground and medical facility, sponsorship, media coverage, equal opportunities or number of sports tournament etc.

Table 2 Availability of Healthy Balance Diet

Gender	Accessibility to Healthy and Balance Diet				Total
	Yes	No	Can't Say	No Response	
Female	119	64	38	13	234
Male	136	24	38	0	198
Total	255 (59.0%)	88 (20.4%)	76 (17.6%)	13 (3.0%)	432 (100.0%)

The above table shows the availability and accessibility of healthy and balance diet to the respondents according to their sports. 255 out 432 respondents of which 119 are female and 136 are male get healthy diet according to their sports required while 88 respondents out of 432 of which 64 are female and 24 are male do not have access healthy and balance diet. 76 out of 432 of which include 38 of female and 38 of male are not sure about whether they have access to healthy diet or not. 13 respondents out of 432 do not respond to this question.

Table 3 Availability of Playing Equipment

Gender	Equipment Availability on time of Practice and Sports Tournament				Total
	Yes	No	Can't Say	No Response	
Female	92	96	28	18	234
Male	113	51	32	2	198
Total	205 (47.5%)	147 (34.0%)	60 (13.9%)	20 (4.6%)	432 (100.0%)

The table-3 shows the accessibility or availability of sports equipments to the respondents while they are performing in sports event or practicing in stadium. 205 out 432 respondents of which 92 are female and 113 are male, has accessibility of equipments whenever they needed as their sports required while 147 respondents out of 432 do not have accessibility to sports equipments. 60 out of 432 of which include 28 of female and 32 of male are not sure about whether they have accessibility of equipment or not. 20 respondents out of 432 do not respond to this question.

The table-4 shows that if the equipments are available to both male and female players so the quality of the equipment to male and female players are comparable or not. 187 out 432 respondents of which 76 are female and 111 are male has the access to equipments and they find it good and equal in quality while 157 respondents out of 432 of which 119 are female and 38 are male who have accessibility to equipment but the quality is not good or comparable. 77 out of 432 of which include 28

6

of female and 49 of male are not sure about whether the quality of the equipment of both male and female player are comparable or not. 11 respondents out of 432 do not respond to this question.

Table 4 Quality of Playing Equipment

Gender	Quality of Equipment of male and female players are comparable				Total
	Yes	No	Can't Say	No Response	
Female	76	119	28	11	234
Male	111	38	49	0	198
Total	187 (43.3%)	157 (36.3%)	77 (17.8%)	11 (2.5%)	432 (100.0%)

Table 5 Availability of Coaching Facility

Gender	Receiving Coaching from a qualified coach				Total
	Yes	No	Can't Say	No Response	
Female	53	148	23	10	234
Male	87	55	56	0	198
Total	140 (32.4%)	203 (47.0%)	79 (18.3%)	10 (2.3%)	432 (100.0%)

The above table shows the gender wise accessibility to coaching facility to the subject.140 out 432 respondents of which 53 are female and 87 are male who are receiving coaching from qualified a coach while 203 respondents out of 432 of which 148 are female and 55 are male who do not have accessibility to the good coaching facility.79 out of 432 of which include 23 of female and 56 of male are not sure about their accessibility of coaching facility. 10 respondents out of 432 do not respond to this question. This shows that in comparison of male respondents female has less access to coaching facility.

Table 6 Satisfaction with Coaching Facility

Gender	Satisfaction with Coaching				Total
	Yes	No	Can't Say	No Response	
Female	60	108	47	19	234
Male	76	52	65	5	198
Total	136 (31.5%)	160 (37.5%)	112 (25.9%)	24 (5.6%)	432 (100.0%)

The above table-6 shows the gender wise satisfaction to coaching facility of the respondents. 136 out of 432 respondents which include 60 female and 76 male are satisfied with their coaches while 160 respondents of which 108 are female and 52 are male not satisfied with their coaches. 24 respondents no respond to this question. This shows that majority of female respondents are not satisfied with their coaches in comparison of their male counterparts.

Table- 7 shows that a majority (246) of respondents are satisfied with their practice time while 82 respondents are not satisfied with their practice time. 17 respondents not respond to this question.

Table 7 Satisfaction with Practice Time

	Are you satisfied with your practice time				
Gender	Yes	No	Can't Say	No Response	Total
Female	103	66	49	16	234
Male	143	16	38	1	198
Total	246 (56.9%)	82 (19.0%)	87 (20.1%)	17 (3.9%)	432 (100.0%)

Figure 1 Equal Quality and Access to Training Facilities

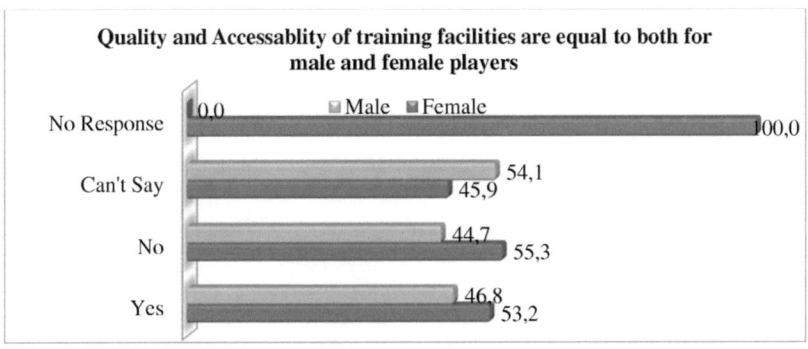

The above figure 1 shows that if the coaching facility is available to both male and female players so the Quality and Accessibility of training is equal to both for male and female players or not. 190 out of 432 respondents of which 53.2% are female and 46.8% are male who are accessing coaching and find the training quality equal for both sexes while 170 respondents out of 432 of which 55.3% are female and 44.7% are male who have accessibility to training but the quality is not good or comparable of both sexes. 61 out of 432 of which include 45.9% of female and 54.1of male are not sure about whether the quality of the training facility of both male and female player are comparable or not. 11 respondents out of 432, no respond to this question.

Table 8 Focus of coaches mainly on male players than female players while practicing and training

Gender	Focus of coaches mainly on male players than female players while practicing and training				Total
	Yes	No	Can't Say	No Response	
Female	154	46	26	8	234
Male	97	48	53	0	198
Total	251 (58.1%)	94 (21.8%)	79 (18.3%)	8 (1.9%)	432 (100.0%)

The above table shows that a higher number of respondents (251 out of 432) are agreeing with the statement that coaches are mainly focuses on male players to improvement of sports techniques rather than female players. 94 out of 432 respondents denied this statement while 79 are not sure which include 26 of female and 53 of male respondents. 8 out of 432 do not respond to this question.

Figure 2 Quality and Accessibility of Medical services is comparable

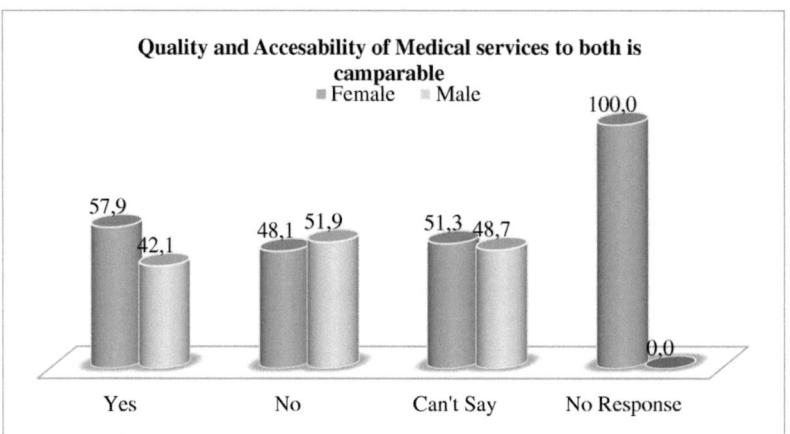

The above figure shows gender wise representation of quality and accessibility of medical services to both sexes for male and female players are equal or not. 183 out 432 respondents of which 57.9% are female and 42.1% are male who are accessing medical facility and find it equal and comparable for both sexes while 162 respondents out of 432 of which 48.1% are female and 51.9% are male who have not find the quality of medical services good or comparable of both sexes. 76 out of 432 of which include 51.3% of female and 48.7% of male are not sure about whether the quality of the medical services of both male and female player are comparable or not. 11 respondents out of 432 do not respond to this question.

FINDINGS & DISCUSSION

1. The study found that a majority of respondents including male sportsperson and female sportspersons has the accessibility to healthy and nutritious diet. In comparison of male sports person female sportsperson have less accessibility to healthy diet which is the foremost requirement of a sportsperson.

2. The study findings shows that majority of respondents has not accessibility to playing equipment on time which they requires while they are practicing for tournaments. In comparison of female sportsperson, male sportsperson have more availability or access to good quality equipment.

3. The present study found majority of respondents including both sexes has no accessibility to the coaching facility.

4. The study also found that majority of respondents including both sexes is satisfied with their equal quality of training.

5. The study found that majority of respondents (183 out 432) is accessing medical facility and find it equal and comparable for both sexes. In comparison of female sportsperson, their male counterparts have less accessibility of good quality medical facility. This shows that there is need to improve the medical facilities and make them more easily accessible to all.

CONCLUSION

The study conclude with the fact that in comparison of their male counterpart female respondents has less accessibility to basic sports facilities due to their gender. They have less access to healthy diet, the availability and quality of playing equipment, medical services for both sexes are not equal. Female respondents have less access to the basic sports facility as compare to their male counterpart. The study concludes that gender matters in the access of sports facilities. In the form of healthy diet, playing equipment, medical facility, coaching facility, training time & quality of training, sponsorship and media coverage female sportsperson face more difficulty as compare to their male counterpart due to their gender.

REFERENCES

Coakley, J. (1982). Sports in Society: Issues and controversies (5th Ed.). St Louis, MO: Mosby.

Coakley, J. (1982). Sports in Society: Issues and Controversies (6th Ed.). Boston: McGraw

Connell, R. W. (1995). Masculinities. Champaign III: Polity Press.

Duncan, M. C., Messner, M. A., Williams, W. and Jensen, K. (1994). Gender Stereotyping in Televised Sports. Los Angeles, US: Amateur Athletic Foundation.

Duncan, M.C. (1990). Sports photographs and sexual difference: Images of women and men in the 1984 and 1988 Olympic Games. Sociology of Sport Journal, 7, 22-43.

"Early Childhood." UNICEF. N.p., 29 Aug. 2007. Web. 15 May 2013.

Eccles, J. S. and Harold, R. D. (1991). Gender Differences in Sport Involvement: applying the Eccles' expectancy value model. Journal of Applied Sport Psychology, 3(1), pp. 7-35.

Engel, A. (1994). Sex Roles and Gender Stereotypes in Young Women's Participation in Sport. Feminism & Psychology, 3, 439-448.

Epstein, D., Kehily, M., Mac and Ghail, M., and Redman, P. (2001). Boys and Girls Come out to Play: making masculinities and femininities in school playgrounds. Men and Masculinities, 4(2), pp. 158-172.

Fasting, K. and Sisjord, M. K. (1985). Gender Roles and Barriers to Participation in Sports. Sociology of Sport Journal, 2, pp. 345-351.

Gill, D. L. (1988) Gender Differences in Competitive Orientation and Sport Participation. International Journal of Sport Psychology, 19, pp. 145-159.

Lenskyj, H. (1987) `Female sexuality and women's sport'. Women's Studies International Forum 10(4), pp. 381-386

YOUR KNOWLEDGE HAS VALUE

- We will publish your bachelor's and master's thesis, essays and papers

- Your own eBook and book - sold worldwide in all relevant shops

- Earn money with each sale

Upload your text at www.GRIN.com and publish for free